5 STEPS TO TAKE TO START ENDING POVERTY & GENERATIONAL CURSES IN THE BLACK COMMUNITY

DOROTHY A. COOPER

ISBN-978-0-578-77221-9

5 Steps To Take To Start Ending Poverty & Generational Curses In The Black Community

Cover Design
Soul Sister Ink

Soul Sister Ink

Katrina'sWorks Publishing LLC

Katrinasworks.com

DEDICATION

To my parents, Jessie Lee Dyson, Sr. and Fannie Francis Dyson, I love you two so much! It has been so hard in life. I wanted to give you both the world! But the fight has been horrific! I understand now Dad.
I understand your cries I heard in the wee hours of the night, Mom, after Dad took sick. I understand and it hurts.

Therefore, with this book, I am writing it with the intent to heal as many families in the Black community, as it will heal, from the same pains our family has endured for generations. The pains associated with poverty and how to beat the daily fight of no longer being under its control. The answers here were well thought out and the wisdom which came with it derived from over 53 years of personal testimony. I wish more than anything, Dad could have found a little peace from knowing his family, his children and their children, wouldn't have to suffer in life the way he did. Getting over the generational hand down of poverty took a lot out of your fight. But you fought Dad, until the end. This

was your biggest concern when the last words spoken to me in my bedroom, which became your death bed, "Get up! Don't stop getting up. It is in the getting up one day you shall get over!"

Thank you Dad! I appreciate you for letting me know you were proud of me as the first female to ever garner the seat of mayor in Turrell, Arkansas. I gave my all in the getting up to make sure the name of Dyson would ring throughout the community for generations to come! Rest in Peace! We love and miss you so!

JESSIE LEE DYSON, SR.

1941-2016

R.I.P

WE LOVE AND MISS YOU!

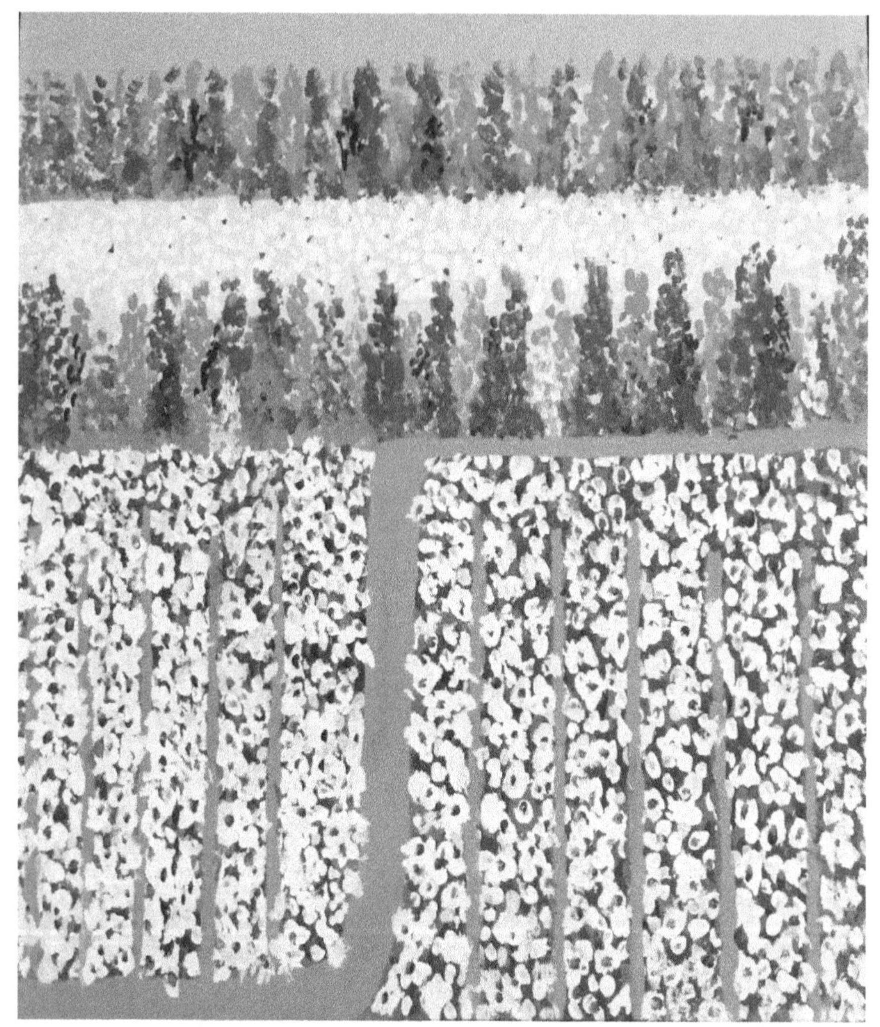

IF COTTON COULD TALK

DOROTHY A. COOPER

ARTIST & AUTHOR

05/05/2017

DEAR MOMMA I LOVE YOU GIRL!
THANK YOU!

First of all,
I am so thankful to still have you here!
Looking great at 78!
I am so grateful for every opportunity granted
To still be able to gaze upon your beauty!
For the lovely picture which my eyes see
Is a poetic and prophetic picture of me...

Dear Momma,
I love you girl! Thank you!
I understand, now, just how difficult
It was on you in 1974 when Dad got sick;
May he continue to Rest in Peace,
It was a battle but you kept your seat
As his wife until the end of his life in 2016
We love and miss you, Dad, so much!
But you hung in thcrc Momma!
For all eight of your children, too,

You have been there Momma.
Have you even had a life of your own?
After, for so many others,
Having to be so strong?

Dear Momma,
I love you girl! Thank you!
I understand, now, why you had to be so tough!
Times were, especially for you, rough!
But through your strength Momma
You raised three girls
To have respect for our "pearls"
And always keep our dresses
Below our knees for that is a jewel
Only husband material should be
Allowed to see! You were right Momma!

And though, it took up a lot of your time,
In your mind, on keeping us girls straight
You have given just as much of you,
Including money, too, to unselfishly find,
The wisdom, knowledge, strength and patience,

Through prayer, to keep five boys in line!
Incredible! So much, in fact, no matter who
The conversation is with
They will be glad to tell of how-
Thank you, yes ma'am, no ma'am, please
Yes sir, no sir, I appreciate you-
Are always words shared
From, not just the lips, but hearts, as well
Of every last one of your children,
Even the one in jail! Thank you Momma!
Oh, and what I wouldn't give to let you have
One more conversation alone with Delone!
Gone too soon!
We miss and love you brother, so much!

Dear Momma,
I understand, now, all of the tears,
As a youngster, my ears woke to hear
You shedding so many late nights!
It makes my eyes cry, now,
To think back on how, every day,
To this very day, you have woke up

With a fight in your spirit
To keep your family together!
You could have given up on us Momma!
But you never did and you never have!
A whole bunch of children have been
Given to other family members and even friends to raise
For similar situations!
But, I, we all, including your children
Children, children, give you praise for how you stayed
To be deemed the perfect definition of Momma!
Simply remarkable you are!

I just want to give you your flowers, Momma
While you can still touch, feel, smell and see them, too!
I, we thank God everyday
For blessing us with a Momma like you!

Dear Momma,
I love you girl!
Thank you!

FANNIE FRANCIS MOORE-DYSON

OUR DEAR MOTHER!

We thank God for our beautiful Queen still

being here to teach and show us the way!

MY MOMMA'S ROSES

DOROTHY A. COOPER

ARTIST & AUTHOR

08/12/2017

INTRODUCTION

There is a pandemic which has been happening in these United States of America and for centuries! It is way worse, as horrific as it is, I am praying for us all, then the paralysis of what Covid-19, according to Google, a mild to severe respiratory illness which is caused by a coronavirus, has caused just in the first few months of 2020. It is currently September, at the printing of this book, and approximately 191,000 Americans, alone, (https://www.cdc.gov) have died from a disease which cannot be seen by the naked eye. It is transmitted chiefly by contact with infectious materials, objects or surfaces contaminated by the causative virus, Google continues. However, as mind boggling and heart wrenching as this pandemic has left the world, if there was comparison done, the number of deaths would fall considerably short to the plague which has killed the Black community as a whole and for centuries!

Throughout the following pages, it is the author's sole intent to provide straightforward avenues, specifically designed to lead to the rejuvenation of the Black community as a whole. A cleaner, healthier community capable of thriving on its own and certainly for many generations to come. The goal of this book will make our ancestors proud, by the unity it will cause in realizing there is no better time than now to work together on the change the dying Black community so desperately needs. Though times were very, very difficult during slavery, we should all easily agree, one positive and constructive thing was left for generations to come to follow was the fact our ancestors worked together to make things happen. Yes, they did. Our ancestors looked out for each other as best they could. Yes, they did. We know this to be true. For if not working to produce what was demanded to be produced, every last one of our ancestors would have been killed by the hands of pure evilness for not producing. This then means there would be no us!

Nonetheless, there is encouragement for all to read these truthful words shared. At the same time, however, let there be understanding, putting them all together is

for the common good of the Black community. Though history will be shared all throughout, it is important to also understand, saving the Black community can only be done by the Black community. We've tried trusting others to get us there with no success. From the outside, support us financially, as it should be, for we have helped everyone else rise to the top in their dealings. Now, we should all easily agree, from all of the constructive changes happening to demolish racism and White supremacy, the world is saying it is the Black community's turn to be treated equally and fairly by being deemed a part of one race here in the United States of America. And that race is the Human Race.

Thank you for your undivided attention as we continue on. To God through the submissive will of Jesus be all glory. ~Amen~

ANCESTORS

CELEBRATING THE END OF POVERTY &

GENERATIONAL CURSES

IN THE BLACK COMMUNITY

DOROTHY A. COOPER, ARTIST AND AUTHOR

9/11/2019

A LITTLE HISTORY

There will be no sugar coating of this book. It will be as short and to the point as possible as God has required it to be. Besides, truth has never needed a long time to be shared. While writing, God provides visions of understanding of where things are and why for the Black community. His speech is soft, deep, but also, truthfully stern. Therefore, this book shall be the same. In fact, God had me to rewrite it three times to assure the truth is

perfectly told and shared here. It is time for healing of the Black community which has been suffering, badly and has been for a very long time, we should all easily agree. We find ourselves at the beginning of change happening for the greater good at this very point in

history. Should there be any positive change taking place, however, in and for the Black community, as a whole, again, we should all easily agree, it is the time now to speak up to make it happen. The Black community cannot afford to fall by the wayside now, in order to make great things happen for the common good of our community!

First, and foremost, it is the responsibility of the entire Black community to save the entire Black community. There can be nothing or no one, no distractions or disturbances, as in the past, to keep the Black community from coming together, God says. It will be a very, very long time before provisions are made again which will cause statues of those deemed as prominent leaders to be removed from sacred places which have represented some of the very hearts who helped to keep Black communities with a "knee" on its neck. Sometimes, both knees, we should all easily, agree.

So many, many prayers, over the last 600 years, and more, have been prayed to bring the hurt and pain, in which was being, plus continues to be, inflicted on the Black community to a halt. Here is one answer. The White community cannot and will not save the Black

community. History has proven this! Right? No one should get mad at the truth for the truth is the only thing which makes all of us free! Repeat, no one can save the Black community but the unifying of the Black community.

As a whole, the White community has only used the Black community, especially, as "slaves", if you will, to keep their community standing in superiority. It has been a historical purpose to this very fact. The United States of America was built off White supremacy. It is the truth! Right? The Black community was not captured, hand tied, enslaved, put deep in the bottom of a ship for months, now, and brought over to live in these United States of America so life would be equal to our captures! No way! Here's the thing, not too much has changed. It is the truth!

The ancestors of the Black community worked their fingers to the bones tirelessly to make sure, without a choice of doing so, everything the White man and his entire family needed was taken care of on a daily basis. The blood, sweat, prayers and tears of the Black

community; chopped the cotton, picked the cotton, raised the food, cooked the food, planted the gardens, built all of the furniture, sewed the curtains, clothes, sheets, tablecloths and even built the elaborate big houses for the White community to get rich, eat well, sleep well and live well, in. All while, get this, the Black community, whole families, now, slept in barns or broken-down huts and shacks on the dirt floor which were hid behind the big nice houses. One of our biggest problems in the Black community today is some of us are starting to think things have changed for the Black community as a whole and it has not.

Every day, past and present, the Black community leaves the brokenness of the Black community to go slave in the White community, for the White business owner. Instead of a field, it is now a factory or building. Same difference. Then the Black community gets off work and go back to the Black Community only to pray for a better way of living in the households of the Black community. Especially in our own households. Huh? That does not even make sense now that God is giving it to me like this as an example. Wow! This cannot continue

to make sense to the Black community, either, and as a whole.

For the most part, it is the educated Black community who feels there is no more suffering in the Black community. Not pointing fingers here, just being honest! Thank God for you! Thank God you made it out of the pandemic happening in the Black community! However, getting educated must never be, as a member of the Black community, seen as an opportunity to forget the Black community. No one can save or uplift the Black community but the Black community. No matter where we are in life, especially if doing what is deemed as "good", we are obligated to every last one of our Ancestors who fought for us to be who and where we are today! Anyone, we should all easily agree, not agreeing with this message is a part of the problem and not the solution!

Now, how can there be so much praying, God says, for shackles to be removed from the Black community when they were removed years ago? We are praying only to not believe what we are praying for. Praying in the Black community and churches has become the same thought as in the White community! A thought of

prosperity by any means necessary. It is the truth! Everything the history of the White community has done in misusing the Black Community in order to get there, has been done only for the uplifting of the entire White community. Right?

There is absolutely nothing at all wrong with desiring to be rich. Especially when putting in the honest work it takes to get there. However, in order for the Black community to see unified prosperity, it is solely up to the Black community to make it happen. History, again, tells us there is no relying on any other group in order to make it happen. We cannot use the White community like the White community has used the Black community to obtain their fortune which still has the capability to be passed from generation to generation. It is impossible! The White community is not going to be a slave for the Black community! Let us face reality here! This is what the Black community is waiting and praying for to happen.

IS IT REALLY PRAYING TIME STILL?

Okay, so the Bible does say in all our ways acknowledge God through the submissive will of Jesus which always can be interpreted as those who follow His ways should continuously pray without ceasing. Let me say this, all through slavery, over a few centuries, now, do we think our ancestors were not praying for a disconnect experienced from being bound by the scars of slavery? Of course they were. This is a topic for a whole other book in itself.

However, in order for us, the Black race, to find ourselves thriving successfully as one race, the human race, we must remember we were brought over to the United States of America tied and bound by the White man. We were not invited of our own freewill. Look how long we have been praying for vengeance on the White man for all of the horrific things done to the Black man,

and still, again, we should all easily agree, not too much has changed.

The reason for this is because, though we, as a Black race, are known for loving to pray and doing so without ceasing, we are also known by other communities to not fully have faith in those things in which we pray for. Meaning the other part of faith, the one with the most significance to make it faith, is to put in the work in which it takes in order to see the prayer become result. It is such a great feeling left to pray. Especially for peace from things which brings the heart no peace. But if the praying is ever to come to fruition, getting off our knees and going to find the peace in which our spirits need must first take place, we should all easily agree.

Therefore, God says, to pray for the spirit of fear to be removed from among the Black community. We are afraid, still, of obtaining what God has for the Black community on our own. Why? When the Black community is the sole reason why America became great in the first place? It is true. We should be proud of our ancestors for all of the hardship they endured so we could have just a little more in these days and time. The

White community, after trying to figure it out themselves here in the USA, heard of how there was a different group of man, over in Africa, who was successfully doing the exact same thing, already, in which the White man was seeking to do, but could not. Read your history books. The ones which leaves out the history of the Black man before slavery.

Because of smartness and the ability to work hard even in scorching hot weather this is why the White man went to Africa and captured the Black man (this includes the Black woman, also) in bondage so these same traits would be used to bring the White community into great prosperity. It worked by placing the spirit of fear in to the Black man. Oh yeah, having to watch another Black person being lynched, having mad dogs released on them, hangings, raping, killed, murdered, being shot at, castrated and burned alive while hanging from a tree, it should cause fear of not wanting it to happen to you. God desires for the Black community to know it is okay now to go beyond the fence to get that good education and job. But He also needs there to be understanding to the fact once strength has been gained to know the way to prosperity, Black community, then we, as a whole are

obligated to come back to the Black community and teach the way to those left behind. It is true.

We, for the most part, say we believe and trust God, through the submissive will of Jesus. But yet our actions say we do not. Fear of coming together to not let anything or anyone stop the uplifting of the Black community by the Black community is our main problem as a Black community. But it does not need to be. The spirit of jealousy is another issue in the Black community. It started with being enslaved, too. Our ancestors were made to fight with our Black Brothers and Sisters for our life simply because the White man needed some entertainment.

Also, sometimes the fight was to be able to even eat. Not only did this cause jealousy among the Black community, it caused hatred too of not desiring to see one family having more than the next. Afraid of one having more than the other. Pray for this type foolishness to be removed and replaced with a spirit of love to consume all hearts of the Black community by the Black community no matter what community we currently reside in. The avenues then provided by God will become easier to see as a whole. Therefore, making it

achievable without great effort and few difficulties to obtain through the labor put in by a unified Black community.

The shackles and restraints placed on the Black community have already been unlocked. However, the heaviness of its weight today stems from still trying to break free by continuing to rely on the same system of White supremacy which placed us in bondage in the first place. That truthful sentence should make no one upset. We must become self-sufficient in these United States of America in order to be viewed as a part of the only race, the human race, of people and all across the world. Our faith, through our working together, should say we can do it!

During a time of uncertainty, a time of tremendous change, a time of great pain happening all throughout the streets of America, especially when it comes to the paralysis of what this virus (some may even say in the form of a president) is bringing, this is the time for the Black community to find that common bond in which so many African American freedom fighters fought, bled and died for. The next few pages will provide the answers carefully thought out so the outcome

will see us standing closer to the "mountaintop" where the land of milk and honey flows for those hearts who work by faith to be there with honesty and integrity leading the way.

MOUNTAINTOP VIEW

DOROTHY A. COOPER

ARTIST 10/01/2018

5 STEPS TO TAKE
TO START ENDING
POVERTY &
GENERATIONAL CURSES
IN THE BLACK COMMUNITY

DOROTHY A. COOPER

TRUTH IS...

"BLACK LIVES WILL NEVER MATTER TO WHITE SUPREMACY AND SYSTEMIC RACISM UNTIL ALL BLACK LIVES FIRST MATTER TO THE ENTIRE BLACK COMMUNITY…

DOROTHY A. COOPER

STEP FIVE

The adults must invest in every person in your direct household. Every last one of the children under the age of 18, especially, should have some type of Life Insurance on them. The more the amount able to afford, contributes to poverty and generational curses ending in that direct family in the case of death of one or more of the family members. This is reality friends. Life Insurance or Accidental Death Insurance, brings about peace of mind and way before death. Those who already have the security can attest to what having insurance brings. Now, this is not the time to be getting upset with the truth being shared here! So, let us look at this very important step with a deeper understanding.

Two things have been proven time and time again. One, life means we were born and two, life means one

day we are surely going to die! It is no secret, in the Black community, many of our Brothers and Sisters, too, are dying constantly, on a daily basis. How they are dying, right now, we should all easily agree, is a different book with a different title to be shared at a different time. With this being said, we have got to be able to have the conservation about death in the Black community just as the conversations are being held now on what to do in case the police stop us so we may have a better chance of not dying. It is understood, this step may seem a little harsh or even difficult to discuss. But death is inevitable and bound to come at some point in all of our lives. We should easily agree to this.

Therefore, priority becomes now, what to do to pay insurance. We have got to look at what is important for the long haul. For the longest, in the Black community, expensive habits have outweighed life insurance. Don't worry, yes, I have this same conversation with my children all of the time. I don't care if the habit just happens to be buying expensive clothes! Which, by the way, means absolutely nothing. Because to wear these clothing still does not stop the

inevitable of death. Right? We are out here looking good but the moment death comes, now our family is stressing even more, in pain even more, at the fact of how they are going to come together and bury you.

One for sure entity who do not discriminate against the Black community, I have come to find, is the carriers of Life Insurance. There is a funeral home in every Black community. Sometimes, two. Why do we think this is? Think about it. Because most Black communities are riddled with crime, poverty, and generational curses which all lead to death. Visiting or calling the local funeral home is where to find out all about the different types and prices of insurance designed to fit each individual pocket. Some policies can be as low as $14.00 a month, if not lower.

If you care about your family, then reach out to the insurance companies today! Contact three or four just to compare the best price for your wallet. Even if it is just enough coverage to pay for burial at the time of death, when it comes, the family is no further in debt or poverty trying to raise the money on their own. Invest in your family! It is what family is for.

One more thing, every Black adult who has made it out of the poverty and the generational curses of what growing up in the Black community had and still has to offer, has a responsibility to invest in their immediate family who are left living in the middle of what the hardship brings. It is why we leave home in the first place is it not? I cannot express this enough. If you grew up African American with a silver spoon in your mouth, so to say, then I am so happy for you! Seriously! That is some awesome stuff. Still, there is an obligation to the Black community for what your ancestors went through for the blessings. In order for us to see the death of poverty and generational curses in the Black community, it is a must we humbly invest, invest, invest, mentally, physically, spiritually, and financially, in the Black community as a Black citizen living in these United States of America.

whole life
underwrite
variable
uninsurable
preferred
rates
smoker
proceeds
clause
rate
tables
expectancy
individual
time value money
quote
group
policy
cash value
LIFE INSURANCE
salary
beneficiary
death benefit
required
term
universal
employee
rider
life
interest
risk
waiver of premium
company
premiums
level
medical exam
claim
benefits

TRUTH IS...

"WHITE SUPREMACY AND
RACISM
DO NOT LIVE IN THE BLACK COMMUNITY.
THE BLACK COMMUNITY LIVES IN
THE BLACK COMMUNITY" ...

DOROTHY A. COOPER

STEP FOUR

The entire Black community as a whole must be transformed. Have we even looked at the despair of our community? How do we expect a person to have hope living in areas considered to be condemned? How is this so when, regardless to our living conditions, we still make it to the polls on election day and vote for representatives who say they have our best interests at heart? How? When at the next election we are being told the same thing but nothing has changed from the last time we were paid for our vote to put this type of behavior in to the seat to represent us.

No more! Our attention, as a whole, even if we know longer live in the hood of the Black community,

must be placed on voting for representatives who live right next to us in the Black community, especially. Representatives who we have seen, way before election time, out in our streets speaking up for equality in our streets! Representatives who have come up with programs and ideas to teach our children of a better way and way before any election. We must change our mindset of voting for family members who have shown not to give a care about the struggles happening in the Black community. Leaders are voted in to various positions to lead conditions up out of poverty and generational curses! Not for conditions to remain the same. I had a rich Black man to tell me to my face once, "No poor person should be running the seat of mayor!" I look right back at him and said, "A lie! For if there is any man or woman who knows the hardship and pain of what the disadvantage goes through, it is someone who is looked upon as poor himself or herself!" Foolishness, I thought. May he Rest in Peace.

So many citizens in Black communities do not even know who represents them in council meetings, Quorum Court meetings, senate meetings, church meetings and any other meetings where the discussions should be the

uplifting of their particular area. Right? Elected officials should be at every meeting vying for the increase of their areas elected over. My goodness! We go to the polls and vote for the best candidate who is going to be the voice for the very ones who voted him or her in to position in the first place! Right?

We have an obligation to know our voice is our vote. There is so much to be commanded when our communities are still seen thriving in poverty and generational curses years after casting our vote. Our unified vote is money for dilapidated communities. We must understand this. This is 2020 and still in most of our Black communities' homelessness is running rapid. Hungriness is running rapid. Crime is running rapid. Death is running rapid. How, when money is allocated through our municipalities for such harsh and unfair conditions?

See, when we go to the polls on Election day and cast a vote, the candidate with the most votes do not just win to say he or she has won. But, all of the votes which were cast to allow him or her to win now becomes the elected officials one vote in the meetings in which he or she will be presiding over. If every elected official is in

their perspective places voting for the good of citizens, why then do we still have so much disdain in and for the Black community?

In this step, allow me to pause here and say, the information being shared comes from a firsthand look. I'm not just some random writer. No! I write as a former mayor elected by voters in a community which is approximately made up of 90% of African American citizens. In my four years, as mayor, the first female mayor in the town's entire history, may I add, attending meetings where funding was being proportioned in the form of grants for small communities struggling financially, was my purpose. I was determined to see my area looking better and flourishing out of poverty! I said no to trash all in ditches and high grass everywhere through being out everyday leading as an example by picking up the trash out of ditches and off streets myself. I did it with barely enough pay! But I was determined to make it and I did!

Not only did my humble work ethics add over $1,700,000.00 in grant funding in the form of a library, newly paved streets, a pneumatic tank with generator to offset an almost ten year old issue of water shutting off to

the entire town, plus a first time ever community park being built, together with so many other amenities being added, it also, saw me working just as hard for 48 communities in my state as the President of the Arkansas Black Mayors Association. I also took it one step further and ran for Arkansas State Senator of District 24 where the racial makeup is almost 58% African American and many communities are having tremendous difficulties staying afloat. I did not win the race, of course, but my fight for the good of all of the people still stands! I worked hard and gave my all only to be voted, even, out the seat as mayor and replaced by a candidate who most of the citizens now love to inform me not only, do they not know, but never even see.

I shared all of that to say, if the desire is to see poverty and generational curses of poverty done away within the Black community; it must first start with our most powerful vote. We must then stay on our elected officials by attending meetings and letting it be known we need help in our falling down communities and for our vote we are asking for change and now! It can be done! It should be done! I am a witness, once it is done poverty and generational curses in the Black community will

begin to be replace with hope of a new day for our next generation to come.

Lastly, take our children to these meetings to instill a sense of pride for their communities. Encourage them to ask questions of their leaders of what new is being

offered for them to look forward to. No one should resist these questions thought of and presented to elected official, especially. Questions should really be asked of the pastor and leaders of the church in the African American neighborhoods. If the objective here is give examples of how to remove poverty and generational curses from the Black community. Then the best way to do so is through the heart of the children in that same community.

MY CHILD HAS A QUESTION

BY

Dorothy A. Cooper, Artist & Author

September 7, 2020

TRUTH IS...

"WHITE SUPREMACY AND
RACISM STILL EXISTS IN THE BLACK COMMUNITY
BECAUSE THE BLACK COMMUNITY
CONTINUES TO GIVE IT POWER TO EXIST IN THE
BLACK
COMMUNITY. IT IS TIME TO UNITE FOR THE
GOOD OF THE BLACK COMMUNITY" ...

DOROTHY A. COOPER

VOTE

STEP THREE

What are we doing? I am being so serious here with this step. Do Black lives really matter? I say yes, but I am having a hard time understanding where we are in today's society. I mean it is so great we have unified and are now out marching with the chant of "Black Lives Matter" on our lips. However, we are just marching to make it known to white supremacy and systemic racism we matter. But wait a minute. Do we not see, as we are marching, we are passing straight by our dead brothers and sisters lying on the street who have been killed at the hands of other Black Brothers and Sisters? Black lives matter though, right? Shouldn't that be no matter who is doing the killing, though? My mind and my heart are greatly puzzled here.

This is such a difficult subject to discuss. But if we are to see poverty and generational curses removed from the Black community, is this not the number one conversation we need to have? What is going on Black Brothers and Sister to make us feel we cannot stop using our hands to kill other Brothers and Sisters? I am so serious here. How can we fix this? How can resolve this? No disrespect. Please know this. I love you all! I am in the fight of resistance with you! But, how can I come out and be with you for understanding of if I step on your toe accidentally, even, the only answer is to kill me without a care in the world.

Black communities are suffering so bad. Young Black children are already hurting having to live in area where harsh living conditions is so hard to adjust to but then to add the sound of gun shots all around as they try to sleep? Is this fair to them? Do we not supposed to care as a Black community? Are we really supposed to just ignore what is happening? All of the cries from the parents who have lost their children to the gun violence. Especially the mothers. Are we supposed to just keep on ignoring it? Please tell me no ma'am. Please tell me we are ready to put down the guns. Don't we have enough to

contend with which is killing our people then to add the gun violence to take us out quicker? I love my people! I love people period. What is the issue is my sincere question here?

Can we please put down the guns and stop fighting? I desire to use my voice to speak up even more for the good of the Black community but it will make things even more difficult to obtain as long as the Black on Black murder keeps happening. What's that? You say you don't understand why I am so concerned about Black on Black murder? Well let me explain even further.

In our Black community, again, younger generations are having to go tremendously without. In some households, this being the year of 2020, there is barely enough food on a daily basis to make sure everyone in the household gets to eat. The Black communities need new housing badly. Right? So many streets in these areas need repairing it is ridiculous. Right? Jobs are needed in the Black community, so those citizens of age to work but have no transportation to get there can get there even if it is by foot. Right? I mean, none of these things will be seen being constructed in the

Black community as long as the sound of gun shots fired are or continues to ring in the air. It is defeating the purpose. Right?

Please do not shoot me. Please do not kill me for coming to the Black neighborhood. I truly desire to talk about and resolve why so much shooting, why so killing in the Black community. I need your cooperation, please, Black community. The obedient sacrifice being made is so we may work together to see our neighborhoods alive and prospering beautifully. Here's the thing. I cannot do it alone. I really need you. Please?

TRUTH IS...

"THE BLACK COMMUNITY IS BEING KILLED, FOR THE MOST PART, BY THE BLOODY HANDS OF THE BLACK COMMUNITY" ...

DOROTHY A. COOPER

"MAYBE WE SHOULD CLOSE OUR EYES"

By: Dorothy A. Cooper, Published Author

Saturday, September 5, 2020

Maybe we should close our eyes,...
Then perhaps, together, we can see
All of the inequality still happening;
To the Black community out in these streets,
After years and years and years and years,
By the hands of racism and white supremacy!

Maybe we should close our eyes!
Then perhaps this way
We can hear with our ears
The sorrowful cries
Of the little Black boys and girls
Night after night after night in this world
Wishing the picture replaying was not real
Of their mother or father or both being killed
Over and over and over in their head
By the hands of evilness!

Then left to lay in their own blood
For hours and hours and hours dead!

Maybe we should close our eyes.
Then perhaps collectively we will listen better
To the pain coming from the inside
By that Black mother and father;
While standing next to their lawyer,
Explaining how bad it hurts
To lose their son or daughter,
Who was just unjustly slaughtered,
Because of their African American skin!

Maybe, nonetheless, we should unify,
Come together and realize,
Before we close our eyes,
As Black Brothers and Sisters,
First, we must see,
Sometimes, that knee and trigger finger
Comes from the same race as me!

Yes, however, universally,

Maybe we should close our eyes.
Because with them opened wide,
Like a mother's walk
After finally being able to put
A crying baby to sleep,
Around this very serious issue

White supremacy and racism
Has continued to creep! Purposefully,
While ignoring the tears
Of the Black community,
Shed for years and years and years and years
Who are now marching these same streets
Seeking change in the form of equality,
By any means necessary, finally!

Yes, maybe we should close our eyes!
Because the darkness seen is a new plan,
One designed to help all understand,
The only way "All Lives Matter"
Is if "Black Lives Matter", first!

Any heart which disagrees

Is a part of the problem.

Maybe we should close our eyes,

Perhaps to see clearly...

~Amen~

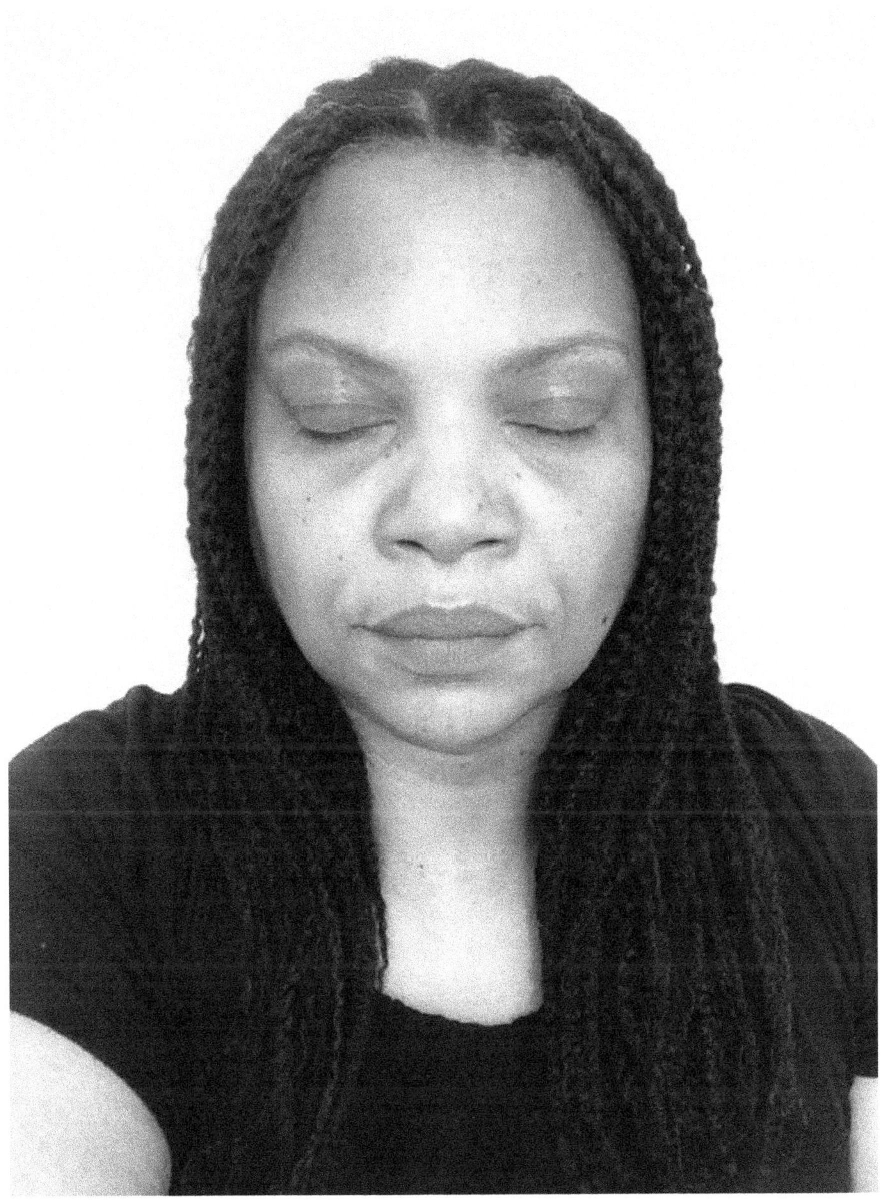

Dorothy A. Cooper, Author

September 2020

"Ye shall know the truth,

and the truth shall make

you free."

JOHN CHAPTER 8:32

KING JAMES VERSION BIBLE

TRUTH IS...

"THE BLACK COMMUNITY IS REALLY WHERE THE LAND OF MILK AND HONEY FLOWS" ...

DOROTHY A. COOPER

STEP TWO

It is time to start investing in our Black children right within the circumference of the Black community. A change from the norm of how we have been investing in them. We as in the adults in the Black community. We must place intense focus on our Black children of tomorrow if they are to be, not just here, but, successful. We must provide avenues which will change the mindset of desiring to be out in these streets causing troubles, to being out in these same streets repairing and overlaying them as supervisors and CEO's of the companies winning bids to repair them.

It is no secret we are in the middle of a horrific pandemic which has caused life as we used to know it to shift tremendously. Our whole way of surviving has changed. A mindset trying to thrive at this day and time the same exact way it did last year in 2019 at the exact time, is a life playing Russian Roulette with its life. Our younger generations who are on this earth right now are the future of the Black community. But do we see the struggle in which most of our children are facing on a daily basis? If our children had to survive without us as their parents right at this very moment, do we think it would be easily done for them? Our children right now are not even attending school normally. Many are missing meals due to this tremendous shift, too. We have got to make it so our Black children may become self-sufficient in the Black community. How do we do this? Great question!

For the most part, children need recreation. Yes, they do! The parks with the basketball goal are great! However, that is the old school way of keeping children constructively occupied. We must start investing in the hands, mindset, present and future of our younger

generations. What do you mean? We must teach the children how to survive, how to critically think, how to stay focus on the moment so the future to come will find our children no longer a victim to poverty and generational curses. We do this by teaching our children different trades.

There are so many places which can be utilized now to hold social distancing classes of learning how to be a carpenter, HVAC representative, plumber, yard maintenance personnel, a mechanic. The girls can learn how to cook for restaurant purposes or clean the house or they can just simply learn with the boys. They can do babysitting and even sewing, too. The objective is to start teaching our children differently, which will provide an income in their pockets. It may not be much at the beginning but it certainly will be more than having nothing!

There are many adults in the Black community already with these skill sets and can utilize them to teach the children what they know. An apprentice, so to say. The church buildings are the perfect area to open doors for teaching space. All of the parks which are closed would work perfectly for carpentry and HVAC training.

Train up a child in the way he or she should go and when they get old, they will remember it! Teaching our Black children these trades on a daily basis and for free are the perfect way to start seeing poverty and generational curses end in the Black community. There is always a house and car needing repaired in the community. Someone is always in need of a babysitter or tutor even. Our elder citizens in the Black community are always in need of help with house chores. What about heating and air? Always needing fixing. Always! This is not difficult to make happen so let us come together for the sake of our children. So much will be instilled in them with this step. So much which will soon cause poverty and generational curses to begin seen ending in the Black community. It all starts and ends with unity!

TRUTH IS...

"IF THE BLACK COMMUNITY KEEPS MAKING THE DECISION TO LEAVE THE BLACK COMMUNITY AND NOT INVEST IN THE BLACK COMMUNITY, SOON THERE WILL BE NO BLACK COMMUNITY TO COME BACK TO" ...

DOROTHY A. COOPER

STEP ONE

There are only two things which must be seen in the Black community in order for it to be categorized as a Black community. No other combination in its majority will work. These two important pieces are the Black man and Black woman. This is a given fact. It does not take a study to see this truthfulness. With this being said, wherefore are thou Black man? Wherefore are thou Black woman?

It is a great and wonderful thing for the Black man and woman who have risen above what the harshness of living in the hood or the Black community has to offer. However, we are leaving and not returning back to save the very foundation which still holds all of our dreams and prayers prayed of getting out and becoming

successful to not to have to return to live. Great! But there is one thing wrong with that statement. If everybody leaves and do not return back to the Black

community, then the Black community soon is seen dying out. Somewhat similar to what we are seeing today.

For any community to be seen thriving prosperously, it takes wealth being cultivated throughout the area, like newly tillage soil, in order to see it producing great harvest time and time again. The land in the Black community cannot till itself. It takes the hands, heart, mind and soul of the Black man's and woman's love for the community to see it being abundantly blessed over and over again. It is that bond, that unity, of the Black man and Black woman in the Black community which is the gold, so to speak, for that community. There can be no form of hatred, bickering or jealousy among the two (disagreement to a point of understanding, yes) least division is what will become seen, like in today's society.

Love who your heart desires. But, also, understand, where the shoes are pulled off is where allegiance lies. Truth is a lot of shoes are being pulled off in households which do not consist of the Black man and Black woman sleeping in the same space. Again, love who your heart desires. But the heart of the Black man and Black woman, no matter where the body is, has an

invisible obligation to its ancestors, first, and then the Black community as a whole. It is true. For the heart to say and fill, it does not mean that particular heart is a part of the problem and not solution.

Come back home Black man! Come back home Black woman! As you go, it should be with the understanding your presence is very much needed. It is a must. God allowed the spirit of seeking success to leave so success could be found. Once captured, He then brings the dreamer right back to the place, where success was dreamed of, to add those things in which his or her heart desired as a youngster, so the next young boy and girl with similar dreams can find hope in one day finding success so they too may return and do the same.

We should all easily agree, the Black community, as a whole, could be doing so much better, if more than just the Black athletes and stars were pouring back in to the Black community. To see poverty and generational curses ending in the Black community, we must, the Black man and Black woman who have left the community to find success, plus the Black man and Black woman who still lives there with dreams of one day

finding prosperity toward a better way of living, must all unite with the common goal of making it happen. Right?

The first thing we must do, because 2020 has showed us a new way of living in this world, is provide avenues to help those of our Brothers and Sisters who have lost their way. If there is a liquor store on every corner, then, let us come home and work to build a facility right beside each of them for alcoholism and drug abuse. Right now, the choice is alcoholism and drug abuse. The intent is to provide a choice without forcing a choice. Most time adults desire to choose life once the choice to do so is given to make by self.

Investing in the whole Black man and Black woman in the Black community is the answer to seeing a Black community thriving free of poverty and generational curses. There is no Black community without the love of Black community.

Together we can change the future of the Black community. I believe!

<u>BLACK COMMUNITY</u>

DOROTHY A. COOPER, ARTIST & AUTHOR

MARCH 25, 2018

BLACK COMMUNITY REPRODUCED

DOROTHY A. COOPER, ARTIST & AUTHOR

APRIL 8, 2018

IN CONCLUSION

Recently, I was asked by a friend, after he learned of me writing this book, "Where do we start?" My answer, saved specifically to answer here, we start in the Black community. If you are Black and have a heart for the Black community, go ahead and start. Even if you start by yourself. Do not worry who is beside you. Just start investing in your community, your hometown. Do not worry what others think. If it is lead from the heart of God then manifestation is sure to come! So just start! Please!

TRUTH IS...

MY NAME IS

DOROTHY A. COOPER

AND I LOVE YOU!

TO MY SIBLINGS

JESSIE JR.

DELONE (RIP)

SHERI

BERDA

JERRY

EDWARD

CASEY

TO ALL OF MY CHILDREN ARIS (TILICIA), ADIDUS (CHASNIE), ANSHEL, ANSHENEIKE (LAREL) & ASHAY'LA, THEIR FATHER, ALONZO

ALL OF OUR GRANDCHILDREN

ALIYAH, ALEXIS, DENZEL (DJ),

ALANNA, OLIVIA, O'JHON,

KYLA

AND GRANDSON AJ (RIP)

I LOVE YOU ALL IMMENSELY!

TO ALL OF MY

NIECES, NEPHEWS, AUNTS,

UNCLES, COUSINS & FRIENDS

I LOVE YOU!

TO EVERY

HEART

MAKING A PURCHASE

OF THIS BOOK

OR ANY OF

MY ORIGINAL WORKS

FROM THE BOTTOM

OF MY HEART

THANK YOU &

I LOVE YOU!

ABOUT THE AUTHOR

Dorothy A. Cooper is a 53 years old mother of five adult children, Aris, Adidus, Anshel, Ansheneike, and Ashayla. She is the first woman in a 137 years history to be elected to the seat as mayor of the city of Turrell, Arkansas.

Dorothy A. Cooper has spent all of her life speaking up for the common good of the Black community. She has held the position of president of the Arkansas Black Mayors Association where the esteemed group consisted of 48 Black mayors across the state of Arkansas.

Dorothy A. Cooper has run in other political races across the state of Arkansas which consists of State Senator of District 24 in 2018, two times for the seat of Crittenden County Quorum Court District 10 in 2015 and 2017 and a re-election for the seat of mayor in Turrell, Arkansas. Cooper is a member of the Crittenden County NAACP and currently is employed as a Legal Assistant/Paralegal with the Bostick Law Firm, PLLC, April Bostick, Esquire, in Memphis, Tennessee.

Cooper's favorite hobbies are drawing art for sell (some are presented throughout this book), writing and spending much quality time as possible with her six grandchildren who all are her heartbeat. Dorothy A. Cooper wants the world to know she has great love for all. However, for obvious reasons, her greatest love lies in seeking equality for the Black community.

www.ingramcontent.com/pod-product-compliance
Lightning Source LLC
LaVergne TN
LVHW012334100826
845148LV00017B/2502

9780578772219